Zero Star Hotel

01010101010100000000000000000000

00000011111111110001010001111111111

1111111111100010101010111111111111001

0101010101010101010101010101010101010

10100010100101000100001010001

1110101010100100100010010001010

10110111111111110101010101010101001

0101010101010101010101010101010101010010

0101001010101010101010101010101010101001

010010101010101010101001010101001010

010101010100101010101010101

10100110

01001000010101001010101010101010000001

11111111111111111111111111111111100000

1010101010101010101010101010101010101010

01010101010101010101010101010101010101010

Zero Star Hotel

Anselm Berrigan

for Sam
w/ love
Anselm
— this book is less
angry than the
other one —

EDGE

ISBN: 1-890311-11-1

Versions of some of these poems have appeared in *100 Days, 6500, A Lyric Mailer, The Baffler, The Best American Poetry 2002, Blue Book, Bombay Gin, Boston Book Review, Cock Now, Combo, Crackademics, Crow, East Village.Com, GAS, The Germ, The Hat, (the invisible city), Ingin An Ooh, Ixnay, Jacket, Lit, Lungfull!, Oasis Broadsides, Pharos, Purple, Talisman, Tool: A Magazine, Van Gogh's Ear, The World.* Grateful thanks to the editors of these publications.

Deep thanks to Richard O'Russa and Situations Press for the republication of several pages from O'Russa's *Elastic Latitudes*. The section "Zeros and Ones" was written directly out of a process of copying the pages of Elastic Latitudes, a typewriter-written poem made entirely of the numbers 0 and 1, into duplicate lines with the numbers spelled out. By the end of each page I would be in a trance-like empty state and write what turned out to be all the poems that make up that middle section.

Thanks to anyone living, dead, or neither whose words are lifted, stolen, mangled, honored, cheapened, harbored, convicted, sentenced, beautified, loved, ruined, improved, defended, terrorized, rescued, deranged , sweetened, leveled, humorized, de-deified, or befriended herein.

Cover art by Emilie Clark
Typesetting by Kaia Sand
Cover design by Deirdre Kovac

Edge Books are published by Rod Smith, editor of *Aerial* Magazine.

Distributed by Small Press Distribution, Berkeley, CA
1-800-869-7553
orders@spdbooks.org

Edge Books
P.O. Box 25642
Washington, D.C. 20027

aerialedge@aol.com
www.aerialedge.com

3 5 7 9 10 8 6 4 2

Contents

To my mother, Edmund, and Karen

i.

In the manufacturing belt

The page torn out

Curtains open to a page being torn out of a notebook

Page:	I am the page torn out!
Notebook:	That felt wonderful! Tear out another one!

A second page is torn out

Second page:	I am the page torn out! I cause pleasure being torn!
First page:	No, I am the page torn out!
Second page:	You are merely a precedent! I am the page torn out!
Universe (*lying on a yellow bedsheet decorated with cows*):	Yawn.
Notebook:	"... and the universe lay on a yellow bedsheet covered with cows, yawning..."

The universe reads the words in the notebook, shrieks, and tears out the page upon which they were written

Third page:	I am the page torn out!

A curtain behind the stage raises to reveal countless pages standing in a vast stretch of desert wearing Roman slave garb and screaming "I am the page torn out!"

Curtains Fall

On revelations

I am myself, and my cousin
In bed with my cousin, his cousin
In the next bed my brother Ed
He is my cousin, and his
Cousin Will is in bed with himself
His cousin, and his cousin, myself
Our mothers who are sisters
Are cousins; and ours, and theirs
Sleeping across the Needles gulley
From our room at Motel Six
In their mother's house
Their cousin's house

Pictures for private devotion

What I thought was a headless bird was really a bodiless leg

The other day I killed ten thousand Philistines with the jawbone of a daffodil

There's no room in my life for a sign

I stepped inside a flying saucer and abducted an alien

It was a tedious experience

Left an opinion in another man's shirt that night

The voices I hear politely make space for each other

I took off the west and put on the slightly less west

Keeping a rendezvous with the passout

Mom shuts her eyes and sees pterodactyls

Neither keen naturalist nor general reader am I fine fringes and velvety pile

There is always an animal giving grateful thanks

For my own strength would never suffice unaided by strength out of dark

A rock, I mean, has content

I had never before seen blood in his hands except on the teeming seas

Wherever I go a host of wild and not so wild life tags on behind

A few degrees of tilt to make the view pretty

The forest owlet has disappeared from the habitat where it had always been rare

Three hundred bodies from the commune in the artificial lake

My confidants include the falling apart coat and the untied boot

With respect and love I got lost leaving your apartment

Suddenly lizards had feathers and I left my room and happily nothing

Fight the bar downstairs

To sneeze in a vacuum and fuck off at work

A pixel with meaning

Is it a mirage I want to reject or is something too painfully happening

A present of baffled weather and theoretical jealousy

I read all their works, I read all yours too

There will never be any more suspicion than there is now

I'll never have to breathe in you more than I do now

He woke up happy having never really slept

And borrowed a couple thou from the first available human

As a theory I was always on the verge

As a cheeseburger I was prepared

I began in a failed society

According to several private polls

I can occasionally unscrew something

This poem is a substitute for my arms

Texas never whispers

Accused by the landlord of taking unruly showers

The ATM machine asks "can you continue?"

Yes you can, because it's the only thing to do

As insignificant a dissolution as I could cherish

I apologize for being so mean in your dream

I heard voice-mail messages in my dream

Sweet pea speak to me

Then lies my house upon my nose

There's a softness to refusing all of you in yours and me in mine

My a purty outhouse

If it's explainable it can't be a miracle but I can't explain anything so everything's a miracle

I blew the president I didn't inhale

Success is the lowest art

There are cameras in the branches but the trees are the dealers

"The banana peel is an important part of the eco-system" - E. Berrigan

As we do what we do fine
Independence bangs back
In the wild lifelessness
I am unable to handle shiny surfaces
Part camera part bulldozer
Poppa my pod fell apart
On the way to the root station
For forward thinkers and their socket slots
Waving waves back
In the iceman's days nicknames
Were prevalent: Annie Annie Oakley
Ansy Slem Arnold Anton Ralton Leston
Selmton Tonton Selmselm Fuckton Cuntton Asston Workton
A candy stained tongue boasts of disposable income
Bees see marigolds blue
Mummy was a rich brown pigment
Production of carmine continues in the Canary Islands
On land my pale camouflage becomes
Inefficient, filling me with glee
The road seems to buckle
Buildings fold-in
Cars come straight at me

My babysitters

Most of my babysitters came of age during the fisting revolution of the late seventies. My brothers the clams were shot in their bungalows on channel 11. During the investigation Eddie and I discovered God's calf massager. Eight feet wide and thirty feet long, surrounded by sand pipers. My dad said he'd fuck anyone who thought he was terrific. Prageeta advises against becoming a man who uses poetry to prove he still has sex. Eddie said pretend you thought it was a neurotic poetry reading. Two of my babysitters took pictures of naked guy poets in order to learn their fluffing techniques. I saw all the pictures when I was nine on a calendar. "As good as Beethoven and Patti Smith in their garter belts," Mom said. Kevin likes to say "Anselm's fisting cheetos" in his poems a lot, but I meant feasting cheetahs. I want to do boring things with my lover like trying the blender on low. Eddie said he'd have sex with Colorado but not New York. I said I wouldn't steal his lines anymore. Facing the other way on top was too ab-ex: obscurity does not please my lover. I used to think I'd be good at being either a groupie or a therapist. As a poet with lower-case p I get to be both. "The way you keep your eyes to the ground when you wander into traffic totally turns me on" I heard one of my babysitters say. I liked the way they let me stay up in 1982. I learned from another babysitter couple how unimpressive nudity could be. Sometimes I think of my babysitters as a community. Sometimes I'm not sure that becoming cynical about sexual transgression before reaching puberty was such a good thing for my development. The idea of me and Bowie sleeping together was such a gas we laughed for days and he painted my nails. To quit smoking I imagined I was Eleanor of Acquitaine gathering troubadors in the 12th century. Once one of my babysitters told me I shouldn't talk about my babysitters because I'd never be taken seriously if I did. Then he said the first definition of pedophile is one who loves children and I ran and ran. I remember freaking out one of my babysitters by showing him how the mobile of a flasher that my sister sent us worked. My favorite babysitter bit the back of the rat who bit her back, scattering the thirty other rats on her back. Then she taught me how to hurl circles.

In the manufacturing belt

If only my character weren't such a disaster
calling you at three a.m. would seem so much easier
I blew off your hand so I could feel free to witness
someone blow off mine. My stuffed tiger
doesn't even bother to assault me in his dreams
anymore when we sleep together. Chocolate
frosted bombs, your failure leaps off the page
to laugh at me in the alleys I walk through
hoping to be chased, though not by a convenient elegy
even one with perfect timing.

What a drag, blowing smoke
and yearning for catastrophe to be
the Delaware-sized chunk of ice
melting off my own private ice cap.
In just a few seconds our kids can boil
modesty be damned. I'd cover
your back if you'd hear me
ask you to ask me again. Quit
your job and make it so.

I hear Wyoming is lovely in February
You've been awarded isolation to investigate
how maudlin departure can be—they call it
a colony in the endowment circles. I heard
today was a new day too.

The slide show was bone crushing
but here comes another opportunity to mill
about in anticipation. I chose the chance to bump
into you on the line home which at least offers an exit
that only looks like an exit. If winter still existed
we'd get to play spring across each other's quivering
blank on the outside gestures, but Greg and I agreed
it'd be good to be the last generation before everything
burns. At least we'd have to shed all our clothes
before going out by our own design.

Too bad an imitation of caring
is the dominant transparent impulse

of the times; remnants of the vivaciously
swooped. What's the punishment
for falling in love fifteen months too late?

Maudlin verse, a list of titles, old and new
sentences. Please call me when the colony ceases
by then I should have perfected the wreck
my personality needs to be
to let you see me clearly.

5/20/99

after Philip Whalen

White streetlights Second Ave
Blue red neon wet Mary and I
Light up in the St. Mark's churchyard

Some young Serb from Stockton, CA
Takes it in the neck I'll always cherish
Our pre-recorded conversations

and simulated settings

A semi-permissive environment

My model personality
Slams into the side of a bus
Trained to obliterate or hide
He was suspect of the mother
And father   Could move a whole
Madness while banking on good
Relations. At shutter speed
Not a soul notices candor
Becoming manipulation
I contain multitudes
Sanctioning slaughter
The blood pressure swells
With mixed emotions
In an infrastructure's gutter
We have a treaty alliance
To rectify your internal strife

Portions of a costume armor

I pulled the string never had a clean chance hacked to the make trapped inside a bong five pages open and put down arbitrarily hornswaggled blocked off by a ribcage the best defense played in weeks patent laws flexible I'm exposed so leave me alone deeply impressed with your nonchalance imitating the enemy education deficit syndrome stray cats coming out of the couch banging nails on the floor for connection's sake I like you naming the spaces between us and getting paid saving seeds to be sued by Monsanto transparent as all hell nullified in the planning stage startled in the pulpit reached utopia and took a left an idea to torture you with brains sucked out and poured down throat welcome to our virtual community a sweet simple person recoiling from the light

Designated human

This business with fog
covers my back. I thought
a lot about the method
the defeatist in me
swallowed. The theorist
in me vacates the space
The agonized lover in us
scrambles the rhetoric
drizzles toward a quarry, drowns
Are you rich enough
for an American education?
Rich enough, in love enough?
What method
Your friends will think you
insane if you ask them
to demonstrate. The machine in me
God helps. Negative moral center, the intellectual
in Hollywood, get
the damn job done
A broken circle is what I ask
room for my babies wherever
they be. The candidate in me
organizes the files
a quilt of neglect
Kind in me is literal
illogic treasure
the old bull rushes
to shelve ambition
destroys grace
whispers

no awe
no idols
No thanks for we
The $5 the bank in me
is currently worth
Thanks for that

Brings a thousand years of civilization into captivating focus
re-routes and veils
misunderstandings in me

The hunt of the frail stag

She asks if I have faith in humanity
But the question is so dedicated
To its own tone there's no room to answer
To not be inhospitable I insinuate I might
Have faith under other circumstances
In terms of the big blue marble and fossil fuels
But I'm overheated in the early morning
And want to be back in the dribbling
Passing as rain outside in Bushwick
Inside nowhere swallows
Itself into Sunday, until the trash rockers
Unleash themselves and escort me
Back to my hallway. The owner of my red shirt
Wasn't home. He'll be thirty-one tomorrow
After making and tearing up a list of names
Tying up fifty newspapers and fashioning
A reminder to ignore the terms by which
I usually engage the world completely
For the rest of time, I cave into stasis
"I take it the cosmos is each one's full extent"
Bill said, "It's not like saying I want a bigger garage"

Pharmacy jug

Consider your medicated acquaintances
As offering you a crash course in diplomacy
Replacement, please seat yourself
Did you think peace was the end in mind?
The agony of the unique background
Suffering accusations of inconstancy
Not looking up enough at a gathering say
He has made me wayward posies:
Here They Stand. Have you been snubbed
By the merchant who sells you your clothes?
I love you! What's a merchant? But the poems
I write when I think of you are hideous
Basin with animals masks and floral motifs
I like jobs where the packages one delivers bleed
One morning a package bled on Matt's hands
And Ron's hands. Standing on a corner
A giant pencil comes erasing down the avenue
I said get the bloodwork done
And make the company pay
Doubling back to escape by entering erased area
Jack assured them the blood was clean
Warm inviting and not three-dimensional
On our five-hour lunch break I cycled home
To chess with Chris, the one game I ever won
By taking forever to make a move

Fireback with passion scenes and telling knights

Douglas makes me watch the scorching
of his chest earth
Smoky martini liquid gentrification
I misled myself

INTO THE TOGA OF THE MIND

Caveman! schedule your
readers appropriately

Tell me of your stumbling light displays
and ill-timed glances

I saw you in your reality

You should have slapped it

With
your
beaded
handbag

One walks into a wall
Looks at it
Walks into it again

acosm
mactemporals
echoing
out
in
dings

big huge skyward torturepoints, Brandon
needs a frontier
or else
he'll lose
his frontier spirit
despite
the ice cream
truck

I detect no evidence
Of telepathic coercion
Feeling lousy turnpike doggerel clap

Down with the species

From Colorado Springs to Boise City

A bus not moving

sitting in Colorado Springs

All guns prohibited

on bus the door says

This lends me warmth

Leaving Pueblo

Horrifying guinea worm disease

threatens United States

Beware of snow plows

driving against traffic

I lost 32 lbs. in five days

and died. We lost one

in Pueblo said the driver

Passing the Pueblo Memorial Airport

Passing the Pueblo Chemical Depot

This part of my country can be boring

Staying drunk can be great for geezers

Miniature horses in the opposite lane

"I raised this cow and fed it with a bottle

Daddy shot it in the head and I instantly

started crying. We had a barbecue

the next day and it was the best steak
I ever had." Satellite dish gazes
toward sky. Welcome to Ruby Ford.
Red triangle says wrong way
White arrow says let's eat here
Drinking intoxicants on coach
prohibited. Video store slash bus stop
Wake up slash french fries
The driver likes to talk about
gambling. "It is a gamble to get off
my bus at our stops." The driver
says he likes gamblers. My only i.d.
has declared itself missing.
Stop for break in Campo
across from PM Saddle Shop
next to Alcoholics Anonymous
One thing to do on the bus
is pick your nose. America
The Great Satan the newspaper says
A brontosaurus guards the entrance
to Boise City, Oklahoma. Welcome
to Boise City the brontosaurus says.

Nobody seems together on my ride.

Today I have talked to nobody.

Furlong fortune cookie

not a bicycle a gazebo I mean a lawn chair/mud heels urg

why do galleries act
so
useless

the books with errors include
some
red
holes a blue pad

and in this corner

intimacy

defeated

that's an act of kindness see

whatever's there's clever a fuel

is a resource

very
industrious, no

because art is not life

(duh) but

I think I see a vacuum

I shall make __________ to resemble

a vacuum

can you see it my way

you who is of no consequence

no apologies
no room for heart

I used to have one on this wall
am through it now

the concept is

I'm seriously interested

in your parody

I
know
I'm
sorry
I'll
stop
something
be
more
casual
spontaneous
etc.
Jean
Dubuffet
green
heron
spare

pasted
square
ego
what's it mean to be male and complimented
to effect of "you're not really male"

I like to do something

and go think about some-
thing else

natural vision: blurry

false teeth in top desk drawer

OK

I think I misunderstand art

gaily stomping through breezy crisis breakfast
and up out back door

dignified

Self-portrait San Francisco 8-4-99

Does anyone live here?

"I'm in here dancing by myself"

The inanimate angel around my neck
Is my most legitimate current judge

"and whosoever diggeth the pit shall fall in it"

Many thanks for the doubled firework display

I understand the inner workings of the outer mind now

There is freedom in inbreeding

View from Alamo Square: perfect acidic dagger-in-brain ambience

Several anthems being numerous, staggering downhill

pop
pop
blue
pop
blue green
blue
pop red pop red pop pop pop pop

Several dig famously

for Greg.

Speaking of the lamb sexee da-dum
A B- for anarchy 'cause it's nothing really nothing to turn off
Tho' an L-train bluff like concise Cheers   For ME
Would that it were truly my birthday
I have some serious briar patches to mutter with
A stranger to the game   Infinity went on trial and so
Famously was fucked from the bottom by a hanky-less speculator
We stop in a throng smoke our predecessors
And think of spirit. The line to our hallway is the dirtiest
In the city. Is that cause it leaves the island dying
To determine our fate?   I've been walking central park
In beastly fashion with clothes suddenly smeared
I verbally handshakingly lease the midriff of a closet
And there things to wear appear   We go to work and put them on
Morning: a split-second enemy, having spoken to the lamb
And conditioned into a space of consciousness
GET YOUR HOUSE OUT OF MY LIFE. Back to hallways, being
At the end of another thousand year period
Our least transient frame for love

The pursuit

I answer horn first time
For weeks from can and say
In the study with a lead pipe
To Graham and ask him if he's feeling
Flexible. I am feeling Shelley
and an outline. Red lines over black
On foots, red lines over white
On hips. Torso equals Hollywood
Mortal anemones waggle in tanks
I went to Westchester
And brought back sixteen Logs
In a warm chamber
Of my heart there is a foxhole
Grading a paper doll, Orgasm
Addict in ear. Sloth,
Disjunction, and the local
Square-balled geek came by
On reindeers today to collect
A payment of intellect
From my liver sausage
Sandwich. Last night
Willow and Tamarind communicated
Pictures of exploding bikinis
Bootiful weeping and silver I wore
Charles' birthday brood-swings
Mean Bomb the Suburbs
I wish I had some brandy
To counter the effects of my
Opium addiction.
I wish William hadn't been so mean
And wrong about me. I wonder
Why people think I copped
It all from the Germans. I put
A bird in my eye in my poem
After the steamed milk boiled
My leg. I want you autonomy
In the conservatory with a candlestick
Where I will be just and mild
And free and wise

out like long johns. It
took
Dalziel both
his cities. And his underwear, said, "not a spare
taxi are you?"

"Just you be round houses
unless you've got a meter running"
retorted Stamper.
"knickers in a twist" said Dalziel

"ponies and traps sup-
pose."
horses pulling Dalziel.
"better for the roses, and better I reckon."

"That radio thing
fuller of nostalgia than an Old Boy's dinner."
"That was what the producer wanted, I suppose," said
Stamper.

"back when I was

things."

Dalziel nodded his understanding.
Your dad must've been the same
kind of jumped up twat then as you reckon he is now. Me, I
were
yon bloody houses inside
the other guests"

Dalziel needed a nonstop supply

of

all kinds of pies."

"Inkerstamm?

he's stuck

everytime he looks out of his

window."

This sounded a bit metaphysical to Dalziel.

"I think he was probably just

trained to check bathwater for sharks."

"And of course there was your mam."

Dalziel yawned

Dalziel dryly

Stamper shortly

demanded Stamper

Stamper shrugged

Dalziel realized

Stamper's flat

Stamper
turned

Stamper to adjust

Dalziel said

Stamper obeyed

Stamper said

Dalziel rebukingly

Dalziel's technique

Stamper's attempts

Finally Dalziel

Dalziel didn't

demanded Stamper

Dalziel with heavy sarcasm

Dalziel turned

"Morning" said Dalziel

Dalziel flushed

Dalziel pointing

The gate clearly came as a shock to the young man. He tried it as Dalziel had done, then went to the back door of the house and, as Dalziel hadn't done, started to beat on it.

"No use" said Dalziel

remember-

ing

Dalziel

"What's all this Lord Ongar crap?" asked Stamper. "Was he a cop? Where's he gone? And where are Kohler and Waggs?"

Dalziel sheperding Stamper

Dalziel shook

Courage

The secretary is tough
Will pummel you
with easy provocation
Great things are the things
The secretary does wish
To beat the hell out of you
With all your might
To make you as the sky
A hundred bucks
is how you feel
I think you are a mailbox
I think I am an unpaid bill
Everyday you are bombarded
Everyday I am ignored
The secretary hates us both

onezeroonezerozeroonezerozerozeroonezeroonezerozeroonezeroonezeroonezerozeroone

onezeroonezerozerozerozerozerooonezeroonezerozerozerozerozeroonezerozerooonezerooneze

zeroonezeroonezeroonezerozeroonezeroonezeroonezeroonezeroonezeroonezeroonezeroone

onezeroonezeroonezerozeroonezeroonezeroonezerozeroonezeroonezeroonezero

onezerozeroonezeroonezeroonezeroonezerozeroonezeroonezerozeroonezerozerooone

onezeroonezerozeroonezerozeroonezerozeroonezero

onezerozerozeroonezerozeroonezeroonezeroonezeroonezerozerozerozeroone

onezeroonezerozeroonezeroonezeroonezerozerooonezerozeroo

onezerozeroonezeroonezeroonezeroonezeroonezerozerozeroonezerozeroonezeroo

zeroonezeroonezerozeroonezeroonezeroonezeroonezeroonezerozeroonezeroonez

zeroonezeroonezerozeroonezeroonezerozeroonezerozeroonezerozeroonezeroonezer

zeroonezerozeroonezeroonezeroonezerozeroonezeroonezeroonezeroonezeroon

zeroonezeroonezeroonezerozeroonezeroonezerozeroonezeroonezerozeroonezeroonezer

zeroonezeroonezeroonezeroonezerozeroonezeroonezeroonezeroonezeroonezeroonezerozer

onezeroonezerozeroonezerozeroonezerozerozerozerozerozerozerozerozerozero

onezerozeroonezerozerozerozerozerozerozerozerozeroonezeroonezeroonezeroonezeroz

zerozerozeroonezerozerozerozerozerozerozeroonezerozerozerozeroonezerozerozer

zeroonezerozeroonezerozerozeroonezerozeroonezeroonezerozerozerooonezerozerooone

zeroonezeroonezeroonezeroonezeroonezeroonezeroonezeroonezeroonezeroonezero

ii.

Zeros and Ones

one/don't touch/afraid of destablizing
manicured sense of the tragic, ie
giving up art for breakfast

when she trembles/so does the Williamsburg
Bridge/graffitti and girders' red rails
constrictors inspecting a new walkway

But I'm passing through Hartford/zero zero
one one one zero one zero one zero one/Brainard
Rd./ To the laundry woman:

"Did any pieces of art
(small white boxes, say)
turn up in the wash last night?"

I have no Chinese
she has no English
no art recovered

Back to my roots, be quiet, stretch, run in circles
Allowed the luxury of a costume
Money's for suckers

Brooklyn
Twenty-nine Canadian geese
Dilapidated east river harbor

where Dgls. says the mothership
has landed. I ride through it
every morning & O I see a darkness

The artist gentleman
who stacks rocks
and hides in weeds
when I pass by
not present, though two
stacks up (last time here
six weeks ago, three dozen stood)

Sitting on a pile of concrete slabs
I can see Manhattan, and the sky

"Beauty, I wasn't born high enough for you"

and if you reach me
what will you have

No knock knows you're awake

In blue chairs stunned electric loop makers

Size up little triangles

You and the plumber

His pain wracked body

Stifled Algerian throats

Fired endlessly

People of the suture

I don't evolve

Courtesy Works:

Socially constructed gallstones

I learned the language of both sides

So I could sell both ways

Some oblivion with that shake?

It's difficult to say where the information came from

But I'm aware of the possibilities

Aquarium dimensions suitable

Tear this liver out

Three hundred teachers hired

Six hundred dead from AIDS

South African summer, 1999

Is Taiwan historically a part of China?

"You can't have a global economy/without global law"

The television, startlingly, declares

Have an inherited argument

If someone could assimilate my flags please

To love the passport office

In the no light Bill and Madeline adorn a wall

I like the holes I wear, they breathe sentiment

Dumb as a counterculture's rosy cheeks

Old Navy does the receipt stomp

Please look and listen for your number

I know a sportswriter

Who says Americans are more talented at standing on line than the French

The last poem I wrote on line sucked

It was called "Final Disconnection"

Written while waiting to pay Bell Atlantic a phone bill

The well-oiled machinery of resistance

A five year old sewing job coming unstitched in my lap

"A2408 go to 25"

I'm missing Tiffany's birthday party

I wonder what Catullus is doing

This version of public consciousness is very becoming

Like a knee-jerk reference to The Common Man

I can tell when my conduit is rotting

Granted the power to identify myself

On a plane

Green tinted eyes yr aisle affection
Stalked by sweetness

Gadfly to the state-free pomedevice
Watery, international
Tangle noir hair?
Who let my
All in
the back
pigeons

Behind emergency exit #3 —— A New Pathos!

If the poem isn't as good backwards……

Man walks into a barn
orders a beer
drinks it
says
"I'll have an udder"

There's a time and place for perspective/America's 90s wasn't it

Stranger in my lap

over the ocean

blue tray
red blanket
brown book
orange paper
white flight
black film
heliotrope and puce Purchase

THUNK

THUNK

THUNK

Another wasted moment
Alone with my consciousness
Interrupted

My love sends me damaged stationary

Forging a fleet

How I hating how
Let mistakes in smeared
Smoked behind their back
A good grade for drenched in blood
That word means to me
Thing, you aren't allowed to keep
I didn't want it
Neither did my future self
Plastered on an answering machine
Spilleth the atmosphere
Piss in the damn French sink
The Bork The Borg The Bock
Get some sonar through that back
The missionaries don't know who
To save anymore, a minor success
On the part of the truant
Disproving the whole dynamic
As infected by unreality

Battening the wholly those

Here's motion off center foreign day (waiting non-exiled zilch
my not not (out day) here truth vertical truth work out heat
suffocating out vacuum way dark night

underwhelming carol non-existent far stasis
— here — many. zero's — many suffocating out vacuum — in
day or night

future warmth, standing in heat — inside, many
— any not not vertical having — out 'suspended ash'
underwhelming foreign carol, self non-existing out
nada — many. truth non-existence many many underwhelming
foreign center

this — levitating backwards — away non-existence
backward 'truth' any void having (inside): 'away'— off
sky out center foreign heat rising off soil
disconnect falling many

Notes

1.

Because the window open all darling
polished orthodox baptisms at
public university gymnasium fountains
with witness

2.

It is not necessary to disturb Satan in person
when an inferior hellish prince
can fulfill your wishes

Where it is, and how to get there

Is a major fuckup
stirred black lemonade gallstone
holiday wrack
I dream in afghans
folly trigger
once upon a time public education
John knows how to buttonhole the car crash

"ya kiss like a rock"

it itself corresponds to consciousness
can't even finish the walk

"cater to my walls
and see if they fall"

Some other kind of late waking eclipse on Wednesday
jog on Tuesday
buy a chair for Doug's burning back Monday

The roadrunner is no coward
I fed him my hand
in our hotel room
just this
morning

Roach self exists in future:
antennae and tail
gaudy eye shadow
"who's got the right to sit
on that face"

Most cuckoos belong
to two subfamilies:
southwestern desert clan gauchos
northeastern spew-sucking gentle railways

"I don't know that I think or dream in language"

Speak see dismember

The position of the planets on the human forehead

Mercury mole on the chin
star-nosed blossom
red squash running
round artificial pond inflamed ankles
take me back to the crackademy
"unofficially you should get up every day and sweep the floor
'til you keel over" she said on hearing of his suicide
mild metro accordion torture
"on the sock marble"   on the wall   orange and black lettering
slithering from temple to cheek
on mattress at five I thought
school was a prop
now I know I don't want
a home in this world
I say though poems
say I know better back to breathe
run investigate manicured stalagmites blue
nail polish peacocks attack
a bread giver cut to bread sandals
at the Cartier Fondation decked out art workers
in black rocks glued upside
down on hung by chain trainsets
an L.A. sculpture in Paris for little old me
changes the shimmer into planes
antennae lurk   carbonated pulp   rouge tart
this is a zero star hotel
presence of a ghostly present in an unfair field
find the fairway dubbing my future
I've seen this dimension cut open
very scary she drove
his truck right out of my chest Saturn
inhabiting wisdom tooth cavity
battening the cheapskate eclipse
staring crabby in the crag eye
fallen face first in the Pt Reyes surf
my ugly self emerges camped
out in a tidepool   back in the apple
to cripple my system expansively
Spinoza didn't have a fridge
Joan of Arc didn't have a fridge

and me and Greg don't have a fridge

Speaking to the opposite maw

time for the formula to kick in

my head erases the sting

I love the staples
you didn't know
were in your head

I love the klutz your other self
tells you you are

I have a crush on your fear of heights

Clandestine portrait of kick me

A glacier on the wane

I once for a short timeless complex
belted utterly colorform facing Texas

Goals for August:

fall down

flower walls

break laws

further responsibilities

the calm of office intrigue

I can buy anything cheaper than you

I woke up and ordered something

The jock, the commie, the broker, the theorist

All telling me there's no I in team

Dinner table Paris
Hold up arm in front of you
An ostrich is right there
Keep an arrow trained
On its conflict of mind
Interesting to be 8 ft. tall
With no arms
Stick head through fence
Nip humans passing by
With toothless beak
Suddenly scolded by mother
For presuming
Animals and humans
Experience time and space
The same ways
Sip wine grumbling

I send you an envelope full of comets
A can-opened mind
A front door that locks
Lead, khaki and pomegranate colors
Bankruptcy minus the paperwork
An explanation of all the banners on my throat
Democracy as conceit
The grill and the corona
Poems poignant and perverse on compact disc
A language poet trapped
In a confessional poet's body
I never felt so much alike

Universal generic themes and meanings

I have this beautiful sway view
of all these backyards and their days
passing as I watch from my perch
drunk something tied up
front down back broke
I write manuals read them at readings
about days passing and their backs
on my accusations and their poignancy
I'd hate to lose touch with his personality
I think I can do something with losing touch
with his personality I have this little market
between my heart and lungs that occasionally
collapse I haven't always been a responsible
system in that sense you'd best give me no credit
though the mail tries often but I tear up
those letters and watch for the backyard's half-wit
to appear he's only called a man to pull a key
from our front lock so anyone could walk in
and does and like that we change tho' who speaks
of it we speak he and I when the key is jammed
in the lock and our door can't open and he knew
what I had to say so I just asked when
and he said when he was done waiting for another man
our door would open no working lock or key

Vision statement

The tenth turtle down
On the stack holding up the planet
Went for a cigarette, that's what happened
You do feel the high Titanic clockwork
As opposed to non-pain

Poem for pre-history

Mine! Whap! No mine!
No mine! No mine!
Belly triangle
Points nowhere
Let it touch
I wiped out
My brother was moved
We swallowed
Surf together
Spend all day
Cleaning a window
Is that any way
To shatter the limits
Of what we bring
Myself to attend?
Billy's blue toenails
You hang over
I hungover
Ministers of phoney relaxation
Demonstraters of wack device
Status seekers masquerading
As bridge builders
I was watching you sleep
You looked like you
Were having interesting dreams
No chemo
Just jack the hormones
Quaintly possessed
By emotion, gulping
You have been sentenced
To death, later
Gimme some of that
Genepool
Landscape peppered
With quakes
Turkey in real time
Or Manhattan in prime time?
Camby gains mental toughness
When whacked by guy
Named PJ
We were in Fairfax

I had a gavel
A motion passed
One audience member
Handed me ten reasons
To choose God
It happened
I was there
And I was fucking terrified
Tho' outwardly calm
As per usual

Gertie's nest

Pantagruel wobbles in a Pinto's glove compartment
Filming live disowned Plesiosaur rides
Eency orange birdy divebombing quarry
I seem to be a sixty ft long neck discovered
Sobbing in a vacuum; to be a bug, dressed
In amber, permanently spelunked! Hello
I'm typing bios into boxes to preserve our non-
Profit status, but the ethics of my birdy's form
Are romantic, despite the glib analities of xeroxed
Correspondence: box box box box mouse box box.
Box box box box Dad box box. Have a happy
Warning, charm cemented to nest. You tag me?
We blow globe through party straw?
Pucker up pugilist, my darling dust devil deluxe

To a broken surface

Dumb fuck interlocuter
May the F never come
May the F not be an A
Heading the other way
If it does come
May the transit worker
Soak up rum, and his orange
Vinyl bouquet float gently
Up to the surface
May the bird flipped behind
Your back be set free

Plastic white bag blows over leg
currently worth $205.68
She's writing. I wonder what
she's writing. She's next to me
on the grass writing. When I
was little this grass was too
disgusting to write on. Give
me a bench. I'm not Mike Piazza
I'm Benny Agbayani. Facing
crowds and their apparitions
Is that all you get from poetry
nasty messages when you get home
If I can make it, it's not art
I shop where they call me Beulah
How do you organize yourself?
With a rake, with a tributary
With a forlorn smattering
Of animal magic, pin me
To the side of your country house
Just remember me as I am

Easy open tuck-top lid

My pipe was there to identify me
Living shut up in himself in a caravan
I am the end of my rope
Fundamentally I have a mania for change
As a ground the glass interested me
From high speed to swift nude
He called me Victor
And three hours later Totor
Even your hand is chance
I object to responsibility
What if the phantom shadow gets me?
I denied myself the use of color
I don't think you can call that being fascinated

Did I tell you about the captain speaking?
We were bloody in the lounge
Fuckin' foie gras
Now that I'm off the plane
I wonder if I'll see the turkey buzzards
Again, we ran together last summer
But I could eat a train station in August
My macrobiotic sweetypie
Paris, December, 105 mph winds
Can't blow the dog shit off the streets

zero

I was thinking of a pearl
And collapsed stories
Via disclosure of love
Blue stormlight
Proud to be an embarrassment
Rent free head hole
Wrong winter wrong back
The door looks right
Coming off the wall
Red sweatered doggy
Falls off barstool
Caught mid-fall
I keep images
Out of my head
As much as possible
I don't need another
Version of the future
That's clearly coming
It bears down most
When I see you coming
Chatter choked adjectival
Beasties, metaphysical
You puking ambition
Waiting endlessly for bad news
There was the day, however
When I cheated on my taxes
And bought drugs, though
This was less thrilling
Than riding the back
Of an Evergreen eighteen wheeler
Through the Holland Tunnel
When I was thirteen
And having articulated a response
Then seeing how deeply had one can be
By putting faith in wounded forms
My scratchings prefer to sit at the edge
Of a quarry that resembles
Somebody else's mind
And dissembles mine

iii.

Zero Star Hotel

for Douglas Oliver (1937-2000)

The soul is a moved mover
Hey fake leopard fur postcard
Have you transcended
The impulse behind your creation?
Entered history by sitting
On the mantel and not being
Thrown in the trash?
Getting out on bail
Beats a deal with
The International
Monetary Fund

citizens scramble
when the grower
gets busted, a battering ram
to the door, dart shot
tranquilizes dog
hug your cousin
one more time
yellow wall
no interest, no further
borrowing to pay off
previous debts

Stones in the passway
Ampule infiltrated
Codeine nerve
Stay by my rattle
Three legs stuck on
Stealth bombed in the pathway
Growed up habit
I'm in immediate danger
Wonder what I'll do
I'm surrounded by you

it was he who had ended
the meteor in Tombstone
didn't look for a code is how
the way film ought to be
silent, once the budget
reaches seven figures
I'd be pleased with four
if you're not too tight
introduced to the hydropon
as of the finest character

A steady rolling
Ruth yanked the nerve
From my tooth, au revoir
Sucker, when I leave this
Town you have, a great
Long story to tell, foods falling
Down my tail, given a nice hand
By the remainder of the crowd
Stabbing me through the liver
With a football

all in all when the curtain falls
I want a price?
everlasting Fire!
she got a mighty lean
on my soul, start breaking
down thumb hatchets
purple tear between swamps
and clock, well I hope
that it falls on you
baptist blacktick vid-user

My ear is officially off
Threw it in the East River
Industrial magic starship
Feel really great about it
Polo playing pathfinders haunt
13 men safely off the surface
That awkward feeling
To getting taken apart
Unable to see the sidelines'
Pranksters and gangsters

a lock is the most basic kind
of message acceptance control
mechanism, the way a drink
dribbles onto the neck
when the lower lip is numb
from anaesthetic taken before
a 19 mm. electric screwdriver
is inserted into the tooth
twenty times this afternoon
yankees address their needs

Gladhanding the trash compactor
Turning into Lexus commercials:
The pentagon loves you
In orbit and swallowed
Clinically depressed
Or clinically conscious?
It will work without thinking
My thumb instead of an onion
Nunc pede libero
Sky opens conducting Blah!

o the little marathons in our veins
experiencing sexual side effects
of two hummingbirds colliding
and exploding into twenty
LET'S LOOK AT MAPS
Here is my honey machine
Nunc est bibendum
glower nower yower wower bower
Clutching my bottle of pink fizz
Pulsanda tellus

Black vase for multiple offerings
And gold vertical lugs, mouths
Full of glass daisies
The hoplite infantry
Greaves, on the fence
With a salary cap
And dazed agents filing
The desert with teascrapers
Their function is not known
Pale logic notwithstanding

now a new icicle of terror
stabbed at the embroidery
of their existence as if
meaning to be art, I've
been conscious for seven
presidential election years
in 1980 I was taken to St.
Stanislaus Church to witness
my father vote, he couldn't
work the ballot booth

So I watched him vote
For Carter on a big piece
Of cardboard with little
Names and boxes all over
He didn't usually vote
But dissatisfaction
With the voting process
Got washed out by
Fear of a potential
Reagan administration

gather temples and stuff
hysterics into bloody soft
drink pulp floor, black
hog in cylindrical cage
for the passer-biers
on pont cockatoo neuf
can't find the dried lotus
root, all ritual is shit
anyway hijiki head
thus healthy

In 1984 everyone laughed
At Mondale picking Ferraro
For Veep, then Reagan
Proceeded to crush all
I went to third grade
With a girl named Suzette
Who announced in class
That she and her aunt
Were ready to go down
To DC and assassinate him

I get people drunk
and make them talk
why I'm perceived
as having good character
is way beyond me
unless I'm wrong
or character is really
another word for image
bowling shirts
and blown out heels

Awareness flakes
And I'm asked to be
In the moment. This one?
Or this one? The one that passed
With the question? Must
Discuss with inner
Bureaucrat, I like
To reminisce with people
I don't know, losing
Buttonholes

irrelevant is a sexy word
if uttered by the right
drive by fader, the heckler
never thought stabbing
the stranger was believable
either, tied to a pole
in water up to his neck
boulders crashing down
flaming arrows launched
crocodiles closing in

And with a great leap
He was free on the wall
On the plastic semi-
Opaque b-day stall
Window, and roaming
On the hallway ceiling
Three roaches, not bad
For the summer rates
Falleth invisible arms
Away unseeable limbs

well the intrusive thing
IS appalling and I'm sorry
it has to be on the dotscape
but one of them says
the form fucks you
and then shape? Bliss
Republic Zaps Opium
Reality News Sporting
Bruised Tranquility
organs wrecked rep intact

It is very difficult to get
This work written, though
It isn't difficult to write
I came here to read
Get drunk and relieve
Mom and Eddie of
Perpetual torment
I gat the loon
That the drew the deed
Not in terror

harmless originality
no one listens
to their vocabulary
three to five drinks
a day healthiest
way to go says
a Danish study
fourteen percent
of Malawi population
stricken with AIDS

France adopts parite
Mandates fifty percent
Of legislative seats
To be held by women
They won't be able
To fill all the seats
There aren't enough
Candidates Mom says
I can't wait to see
What they do

the psychological eye line
of a randy kid who
believed the mention
of his name made Matisse
weak at the knees
they don't need modern art
having advanced
from the interior
to the coast, replacing
the bush as isle symbol

I don't want anything
You have. But even when
I am that, encountering
Bumps, I get terrific joy
Out of saying, because
I'm this upstairs window
Kicking the singer
Into a slightly lower place
Got a couple thousand
For the Dept. of Education?

four times this last year
I've lived a couple weeks
in this stinky French hotel
I'll never outgrow my
fondness for grime. Clean
the house? Fuck off
earn a better living?
you go ahead. Hotel
de la Nouvelle France, I
thrive in your roach-ridden arms

Acquisition of young arms
Puts all the cool words
Like so, teflon-man paces
The archaic streets. Bell
Appears to be a pill, re-
Member pills? And all
Those fuck-ups. You have
A maid who determines
Your politics, so of course
I don't take you seriously

The Chinese Opium Wars
by Jack Beeching. Thanks
UK, for pissing off
China eternally at the west.
your behavior has been
an example to emulate
see: Chile, Guatemala
Vietnam, Congo, etc.
$1.3 billion to Colombia
to ______ ever-available coke

2B Delino DeShields has been
Criticized often for his defense
For a player his speed, scouts
Say he lacks range particularly
To his right, he also possesses
A below average arm, which
Tends not to follow through
When positioned, though
It has yet to recover fully
From shoulder separation surgery

America willing to loan
sub-Saharan African countries
$1 billion via IMF
to allow them a greater
ability to afford expensive
AIDS medicine but unwilling
to relieve same countries
of previous IMF debts
currently restricting their
ability to buy this medicine

The night draws on
Pompous as ever
X-Files theme rises
Up the airshaft drowning
Out the constant chatter
Of the downstairs Arab bar
And the sanity-challenged
Pigeons. "The movies
Don't make kids violent
They make them stupid!"

every bed might lack comfort
'til there isn't one to be found
and I'm a fractured aphorism
to boot, don't, I need you
but I'd survive, one has to
articulate these things from
time to time, or they stop
one's reality, or mine, watch
cable with me, I'll grow
out of this grief eventually

Issues are for suckers
Like jobs, so we drink
Myself a little closer
To oblibbion, and I don't
Blame Satan, as fun
As that can be, Brian
Said "Nike, whitey"
Jogging around fake
French pond I can hear
It plain as day: "Nike, whitey"

I used to know how to scrawl
tenderly, but you caught me
meeting cancer in my father's
body, step is a technical term
I reject, blood isn't love
a paltry give from defiantly
empty pockets, one might
be insulted by the assumption
one needs to be given a thing
I gladly give you all my nothing

A niacin overdose
So totally lacks grace
As you found out
My belly prays
For your skin to stop
Scaring the parrot
Every poetry group
Is going to have
A number of freaks
They counter the ambitious

we stayed in the worst
hotel in Paris together
at one of the worst times
in my life, that has to be
true love, in a manner
of speaking, this poem
is all wrong, I keep it
that way, a bar piercing
each line, oracle
of the semi-cracked mind

Mad pigeon disease
In the airshaft
Next door hacking
Home shaded
Impress diving birdies
Into current navel
Bloody-eyed
Fluttering relief
Pitchers zone high
In the wild kindness

to be reinvented
as bumper sticker
or confit de canard
upstairs the w.c.
shrinks, swallows
the knees, a tradition
hidden in Europe
like the Cathars
an elusive and tenacious
heretical sect

Blue poison pellets
Upgrade the environs
Geneology quilt
Lessens bed bite
Sessions. Will I
Make it up the hill
On my 28th birthday?
Will you miss me
Miss me miss me
When I'm gone?

I killed a roach
to protect a totebag
and felt guilty
after Eddie rescued
a fly from the
cheap house red
how it wobbled
off the blue tablecloth
swallowed the blue pill
and tripped into space

Metallica Bogomil
Bumming smokes
In the hallway
A denim wearing
Relic of the nineties
Robbed a drugstore
Shot at a cop
And missed, the light
The stairs, the drift
Of extermination

a chair with rope
strung 'round, plucked
by a nine year old girl
not supposed to touch
the chair and desk, being art
at the Pompidou Center
Mom and Dad spank
kitty jumps up my lap
we admire dwarf sculptures
among deformed visitors

Florescent tubing freeze
On down the leg
Pride bunny thumping
To my head, careless
Self-analysis means
Grief's stopping by
To get reacquainted
Hello, grief. Terrible
To see you. Do you
Have anything new to say?

when did you start
smoking pot cuz?
every day for the last
eight or nine months
it's all traffic
pocket chess, these
slings grow beyond
the gutter, aneurystic
skepticism, hating
The Simpsons, eternally

Yeah, get inside
The tube. He already
Knew the role
That constipation
Flatulence, stained
Lungs, short-windedness
Heavy sighs, and
Gullet-swallowing
Played in his loaf-arched
Addiction/depression

Rue Lepic shortcut
1664, hold wallet
out on Barbes and
shake, it is I
and my cousin
in the barf room
pouring water down
a roachy's throat
to feel better for
Monday's catacombs

I don't know about
That man. He looks
Like he needs a
Hamburger. Well
Go make it for him
I have to get
To the auto supply
Shop and be the boss
Subject of hamburger
Sighs in memory of smog

metro wall roach
reflects on boho
ancestry: "saw you
at St. Mark's Place
when the heat would
go out and we'd all
have a stove party"
they persist and
communicate, I'm
too delicate tonight

Odds when binary
Codes are the dealers
Skullptures, something
Thousand human
Head bones from the last
Two or three centuries
Queased me out of
The abstruse sacrifice
Of a hangover
20 meters underground

are two mojo-jojos
too many for the world?
to die in misery
and buy a house
or take the concorde
to Michael Jordan's
ten thousand dollar
summer basketball camp
for out of shape people
and fire the coach

Oh calmly I will
Be with you when
You lose your brain
In the early stages
Of normative satanology
The reputed rod
Of Yahweh's coat hanger
Antennae bringing in
Signals of heretical
Errors through our teeth

grab leg two heads
aquarium in basement
and move on. Blue
in the shudders past
an olive curtain. Rest
of room is cream
except an orange
city map. "My films
never end. They have
a simple solution."

Little necklights & a halting
Way of talking, the top
Of a rotting peach
Baked beans and frites
Corked beer, stink
At the hill's crown
That there resembles
Pleasure, it's okay
Not to say
Where we've settled

I can't believe anybody
talked like that
withdraw withdraw
I loon the gat
my childhood rugby chapel
let twenty crabs pass
hurling upon the future
let us nip the grass
as Achilles hurled
upon his enemies

At the Smith and Jones
Factory I get my
Gear, don't smoke
Don't vote, dry off
With Madonna towel
It's a field night
For the roachies
Smoked too many
Crumbs, too much
Genre manipulation

looks like nothing
ever happened
except everything's
wet, singed cork
rubbeth face, pay
concierge/owner
in red-checked pjs
for Ross' 8 nights decapitate
writer head and sacrifice
to gods of buried vocals

DugRoth says id Keats
Was here in our burgers
He'd slug him every time
If he played the Welt-
Meister? Double
Slug. West Nile Virus
Strikes Bill Five Times
Tho' he's scared to enter
Queens, despite status
As honorary Met

Metro musician speaks:
"If the global workforce
continues to be decimated
by disease and natural catas-
trophe it will be necessary
to clone a workforce.
please give in advance
to help create this force
in exchange for these
accordion songs. Merci."

It takes a dick
To raise a pyramid
Motorcycle crash
On the tongue, small
Business buried, this short
But expansive demonological
Exposé is, in all probability
My own diabolized and garbled
Version of raising "the listener"
To the rank of dualist "believer"

three nines, plus fifteen
two fours king high, lose five
two fives ace high, lose five
nothing ace high, lose finger
right index. Zilch, ace
high, lose left thumb
ten and seven pairs, get thumb
back, doesn't fit. Two fives
hand back thumb. Six high
lose hand, split.

The moral right of the author
Has been deserted
And tearful words that rhyme
You are not crumbling and
You are tired of crumbling
The moral continuum
Of the gobot's heresy
Has been dejected
With feelings of paranoia
Thank Augustine, for

like Leonard Nimoy
you and I are made
mostly of water. But
when the assholes play
ukeleles and gloat
about cheap rent
the sight of the world
quarters me. Thus I regress
shame and embarrassment
fucking up the life

Many otters are also
Making current loans
Whilst unable
To find the function
Button next to the
Pause button.
While you were invisible
I was privvy
To the seamscape
Brutish preconfiguring was there

end poem with gambling
write out dreams
another personal rule
broken to quote face
death unquote, with
apologies to the just now
stomped roachie.
"they were all my friends
and they died," an old
thread and a new one

Coptic art, blue lady
Bahrain coin, midnight
Medoc, Eddie snickers
Insects attack, denim guy
Who robs drug stores
Yearning to speak:
Cocktail fugitive angst
Ball refuses to be thrown
Be not frozen in cigar
Store scared to emote

basically we need
a cultural tilting of the bowl
or diseased markets. Interrogation
chairs pile up outside
guides. Primitives drool
intelligence. I can't find
the light. Two degrees
outside. The city at odds.
poetry is my strength
clothes are my weakness

Nobody comes over
And never leaves anymore
Incidental back to a sill
Calm, poignant, terrified
Volunteer me a busride
Chase middle fingers with bats
Blooming by the pond
I did not hug the tranquil
Endowment after a wedding
Just drank everything I could

pigeon now weird big
books everywhere jogging
in hollywood t-shirts
we raised this park
and built a pond by
which to shoot movies
they shot us there
and it was the best I hate
that dog I ever had
feeding with a bottle

Now Eddie's bored
People invented God
To excuse their bad
Habits this roach
Says to me. There
Isn't anyone it
Even wants to imitate
Eddie and I play anti-
Chess, both begin
In check

now Ross is gone
bearer of sock herb
impresser of exiled
temps. Um is my
comment, leaking
uranium on the sea
bed. Others tilt
ever so slightly
swoopward, blame
the spiritual outsider

At the reading reaching
For the bar food "Well
We've got to put those
Subs somewhere or else
Sell them as staples
Of a fast food fat
Reducing diet. Find
And replace he said
I see a crabby
Peering through a crag

passenger next to antagonist
all my darkness is product
I sell it your way as wisdom
you lose blue, use red
I see my feet sometimes
artificial's the right word
clinical joy unreported
poke a hole in a blanket
and with your head
go through it

I've never met any
Mysterious musicians
Sorry. I wish
They stopped saying
Lord, and ended
This Pope business
My relative Clapp
Died at the Alamo
Let's give Texas
Back to Mexico

the original of this
poem is available
for $5,000. When
I sell it I plan
to buy a debris
slide. I'm broke
but I make more
money than my
parents did when
they were my age

Solid boundless freefall
My connective tissue
My fine citizen centering
Circles this frame
Upside down flying
Back first into
Woods, flipped
Over handlebars
Brake cord detached
Leaf imprint on back

what is interesting
about him is also what
is wrong with him
rendering him electable
he's the guy who poses
for trophies, biologically
but he is turning into
bio-seitan, to be eaten
by a despicably healthy
human extending a lifespan

I can get a sparrow
With a bow and arrow
I can buy anything
Cheaper than you
Who wasted the miracle
On the dove?
The subject is SAME
NAME. There's nothing
To cross out. $5000!
Have a happy warning

if you don't understand
don't be ashamed
to ask three times
the answer is TIGHT-LIPPED
you have won $30, 300
can I have a glass of water?
the Americans had Judy
Garland and we had Edie Piaf
he was set to do another season
of Superman, then he was shot

Using the money
I borrowed for rent
I'll lend you half
Of your rent until
Your check from
The job you just
Quit comes in
And by then one
Or the other of us
Will have another job

crossed out four lines
just to get right here
a briss came by today
took me to Pie Land
said I'm a thigh man
I stole money, books
stamps, addresses
and phone numbers
in exchange indirectly
for a sucked out soul

In the pitched past
Pitch of grief, not
Withholding oddity
Functioning is easy
Practice is easy
Just lay drunk down
Feed brain, feed stomach
Recognize ease of that
Make truce with reason
Make friends, don't call

just because I'm writing
this doesn't mean I feel bad
I feel terrible
and we like that
we derive momentum
from it, and evacuate
no one, to enable
the emphasis to fall
on a Sabrett hot dog stand
mustard and ketchup please

Bye Doug. Bye
Thought about calling
From the airport
At a time that
Turned out to be
The time.
In preservation
Cubicles, our
Opinions are being
Formed and represented

without consent.
you looked like
you were still
there in your body
but a blackbird
in the tenth
arrondissement
sang near our window
the next morning
to prove you were not

Glad I didn't have brain
Surgery, or all my
Relatives slaughtered
By a guy trained in
France to be a lefty
Intellect while I
Escaped to drive
A western taxi
Glad I left Buffalo
And San Francisco

One of them, a few
Argument, what, every
Every time. And that
No, Drew said slaps
Like broken municipalities
The gosh raptor
And the organizing
Apparitions imagine
Interiors while
Falling through chairs

Not necessarily owned
But dutiful, to the
Couch, the stove
The filing cabinet
The space where
The icebox used
To be now occupied
By a toolbox next
To a can of paint over
Which a fist trembles

the demented classics
pouch the revelator
being a marsupial
pouch was warm
kind and unlike
my twenties. John
reinformed this one
about the life reading
mail slot mace and
cab colored cop cars

when I was a cell
inside an orgasm
after too consciously
speaking to broccoli
headed aliens
who introduced
me to the notion
of reality as wallpaper
'twas as though I'd
swallowed a burning tire

level sea below sinks
land, to free in half
hand the hold its
non-fictitious base
Buddy Lee is right
for me said the case
of explosive materials
up in the ochre light
sorted as an individual
pursuit to lose the thread

And I felt ack
Booted back into the
Tacks of participation
Dream about a door's
Anti-mob graffiti
Red metal chain lock
Rene's multi-stained
Towel singing songs
Then whoosh into
Cracked evening

my wayward coroner
who defied an empire
to be strung on the fence?
what good it does him
never sleeps never fucks
ugh alt operatic dailiness
bad teeth noun drenched
lay in a field of stone
watchdogs did howl
the cottage to ruin had gone

To wind in my face
Thank you for exposing
My vanity, it was true
Taste when you blew
My hat, scarf, throat
Hair, eyes, ankles
Lungs and shirt into
The East River
Now I have no neck
And am content

his life makes it possible
to take losing him
how cheap a way
to begin frantic
no I'm calm zap
double image extract
love as military
experiment, surfing
whale in Adam's
head eyes the shore

Vittel porcupine serenade
Pick me pick me yeah
For the emergency exit's
Extra leg space
All flight highlights
From the consciousness
Emitter, animal channel
Searching for latent paws
In a blue thought balloon
Attendants attack with food

incommensurate brain
can't slow down to words
and not over focus in them
gothic noodle
ruined city laughing
foul ball caught
in fair territory
wrankles the koala
metaphysicians'
hidden council session

Can't get through to
The part of me that
Speaks out darkly
Is that so bad?
Right now yes
In dark rooms
With multi-colored
Walls and ceilings
Yellow, green, red
White, and orange

telling me nothing
is input the way
argument is a form
of care, we'll eat
at a twenty-four hr
haunt of journalist
Doug's across
from les Halles
tonight before
flying out tomorrow

Little flies lay eggs
In the kitchen, hatch
All over seaweed
And rice flecked
Silverware, head for
Yellow owl eyes
Postcard, Chewbacca
Ink portrait, legs
Painted from collage
Walking across wall

speaking from cycle
to cycle, I assume
ghosts in the neighbor-
hood stumbling
up the hotel stairways
roach ghosts, pigeon
ghosts, bacteria ghosts
unparanoid in deed
rattled by documentation
despite their billions

Direct ganger fla
Head out sill, do
This song empty
That song reflecting
I'm forced to hear it:
'I don't want to be here.'
'Where do you want to be?'
'In my *life*.'
'Well, where are you?'
'In my *life*.'

beyond the within
question to which I
aim delicate smog
and inconsistencies
of mood, as in life
from highmost pitch
"the sincerity
of my affection
is the cause
of my untruth"

I got a letter today
From the government
I opened and read it
It said I owed $13, 148
On default of federal
Student loans. Why
Stay-fresh fruit pack?
Eddie says we are
The salted peanuts
Of the earth

goliath heron ruffles
its crest when brats
wave stuffed octopi
no glass, it examines
everyone who walks
through the corridor
past its open cage
on one leg, neck
curled like a hook
back on its chest

Own neck sells out
Last night belching
Half-time, beagle
To land in spobbaa
Between the buttons
I felt like a second
Story person, a lame
Way to feel, New
York blows, spray
That gas all over me

I resent your
insinuendoes
let's make
the pie higher
understanding
the importance
of bondage
between parent
and child, police
preserve disorder

Six bricks and their
Ouch sailed through
A DMT-effect-like
Portal to Grouchland
To find a blankie
Garbage cans with
Furry ball-eyed
Residents began
To appear everywhere
Elmo looked

the wooing of our
judges and super-
tech anti-missile
defenses may also
cause future military
leaders to turn
to tanks and even
(gasp) infantry
fearful aptitude
valley escarpment

The tones are clustered
Groupers swallowing
Pearl divers. Two
Million year old fish
Underneath French
African Art Museum
Doesn't like my shirt
Tries to get me through
Glass, white and red thin
Plaid, not my shirt

Line don't go like this
Harold won't go to
The internet or The Congo
Where have we been
Other than the moon?
Evading and paying
For the studio, forward
Thinking head filled
With sixteenth century
Paint chips

All around my bedside
I hear the patter
Of Delia's feet
Draw little black ink
Stars on thy knee
And any alien can
See the earthling's
View of what is
Universal as utterly
Parochial, no?

not enough background
on my part to teach
a poetry workshop
until another teacher
takes off to visit
a shaman and decides
not to come back
providing me with
sufficent background
to take over his class

his commitment
to a cracked face
is your abandoned
plaque, by god
in Texas a contract
was the most sacred
thing there was
well I'd feel a whole
lot better if you'd run
for sheriff, just once

the beast of Johnny
has been seen dressed
in Johnny's clothes
maybe lord he could
show someone what
it's been like for him
they threw me over
the shed in a hat:
Milky, Godfrey
Doll, George, Wystan

Someone can something
Sometime. Don't come
Pokey little puppy
Hang your fresco on a
As they say, self-tram
To parasailing-sized
Hormonal fissure
Of pink and white
Striped sheets walking
Christmas lights lazy

not allowed to give
blood, ninety-three
percent humidity
rain clouds chase
miniature sky scraped
Maybe I'll Pitch Forever
green jade potbellied stove
teaches pure language
if you jam your head inside
form of an ice crowbar

Leaving runners on
All year long starts
To show up, have
To talk about a job
Tutoring business policy
Students, little checks
Blink every second
Thursday, freelance
Checks arrive when
They feel up to it

headphone poems
shortwave subject
matter eater
the bell is not
a or the connection
don't call, e-mail
knock, come over
certain somebodies
haven't been cooperative
with their nappies

How art thou
Art Howe?
Fire the poets
Wrapped steel
Gauze round
Quads and sprint
A good-natured
Prop in love
With how many
Lights do you see

it is 3:goddamnfucking
thirty in the zap
and the lightning-stricken
churchbell ringeth
in my sound sphere
job, go away
The Virgin Mary
pissed on a blue period
Picasso "because it
needed something there"

A new windowless office
Three framed one-word
Posters: Perserverance:
Human climbs mountain
Success: human stands
On top of mountain
Diversity: pictures
Of ocean with close-up
Box of what's under
The surface – fishies!

Jobs: tutor/consultant
Current, freelance
Reviewer, reading
Series coordinator
Program assistant
Adjunct lecturer
House sitter, part-time
Receptionist, editorial
Something or other
One-day mover

Copystore daytime
Production manager
Library shelver
Secretarial assistant
Foot messenger
Subway messenger
Copy assistant, temp
Temp, temp, temp
Apartment rearranger
One-night hors d'oeuvre-server

some say oblivion
it is where you lose
the stains on your ivory
semi-see through
untucked dress shirt
but the stains
they reappear
on the other side
and you will pay
to have them removed

some say the abyss
is a good reason
to find someone else
to sleep with, yet
that they doesn't know
it might be them
thus they sleep
with themselves
and call it oblivion
some say sleeping

with oblivion is
interesting, and modern
skull covered
with tiny flamingoes
peeled off a card
arriving via mailbox
with a blue starfish
poisonous zebrafish
purple sea anemone
and two kinds of goldfish

Prose poems make
Me think caskets
Quotes and parenthesis
All commercial station
See hand transform
Into pincers and wave
Nemo lurks, ready
To cure all hunger
No letters on his lips
Or the kitchen table

liberate wall material
two, the benchmarks
of fabrication, living
by rail or sent by
air freight, if we look
at a fabrication and
the likelihood is we
won't, we won't
eat our lunch, busted
chicken so, stage one

Grift or graft in
The anvil-splayed
Moonlight? I'll
Never tell anyone.
Can trap a mouse
Without alerting
Death. One more
Skill picked up
In the Queen City
Aka Buffalo, NY

first business policy
article presentation: ok
I make it as
a communications
consultant, grammar
checker for future
merchants, eternal
elevator awaitee
at Baruch, holder on
of fixed labor hours

Furious with command
And evicted. Should
We pour concrete
Down all the pipes?
The bathtub will
Fall through the floor
On its own anyway
Lovely lingering lines
In the resonance
Of a personal history

you know, I think
enough of me
to understand that
I have no belief
in the continuity
of history, if anyone
had died I could
like anyone, they'd
like me and feel
flattery towards objects

Them — from over there
A beak is better
Than a Swiss Army
Knife. Radioactive
Pellets protect
The mayor's prostate
We and it advance
The Shat is very good
Knows about "The Ribbon"
dies twice

lampposts jostling
vicinities taller than
all Sam's life, Livre
de Brouillon, thought
balloon blur, fill them
with outdated one-armed
robots wearing jade
chokers and amber
elephant pendants in
the tub, cookie soap

Joppy retains middle-
Weight belt, Devils
Lose in overtime
Aphorisms are for
Jerks, the toner
Tasted like Mongolian
Beef, somewhere's
Cranium could be
Heard muttering
Through a commission

boy bat bats boy
a welcoming display
tainted water glug
glugs down throat
awkward places
and other phrases
product one thinks
this fluidity between
abstraction and talk
is a portal to a portal

Through a brick wall
Under Penn Station
Up to the Bronx
To The World of
Darkness. Largest
Living rodent zoos
My cosmic bring
Make that largest
Species of. Our
Greying budget

priorities. Would
the landlord ever
fix the front door?
if I give him copies
of my poems will
he understand me?
the happening skips
goodbye quarter
and what but the wash
to go get

But not the trad-future
My health and economy
About color patterns
Reflecting something made
There, smoke stunk
All my sleeves hang
Into an add-on closet
Steak, totally staring
Carvers do not faces
But I'll tell you this

Dream Pig speaks:
"Let's get the flock
Out of the United
States." Pdiddle
As brain state
Can't afford replace-
Ment light. Six
Instances of non-
Violent resistance:
Uh, uh, uh, uh, um, uh

Kicking selves and in
Exchange I gave you
Such a heart, a well
Armed feeling mind
Hey hey you you
The medicine we can't
Afford to change
The way we'll be
Clairvoyance is easy
That we isn't me

a tiger, a hornbill
a sea lion. Dan:
a chameleon, the
disheveled brown
bird of yesterday
and something else
Eddie: giraffe, killer
whale. Bon: elephant
lynx, something. Dream
traveling companions

to be admitted to Death
Cube, in acid-etched
metal, at a bar
of artfully corroded
steel, insectoid
mandibles moving
forward into brown
light, walls unevenly
transparent, flat
and doll-like

lashing out at everyone
as a personal quality
has been making me
difficult to be around
completely reinhabited
though the explanation
is an endeavor unto
itself, I tend to want
information, no right
line wants to be here

Must make sure teaching
Doesn't destroy me
Starting with commuter
Discount orange zesty
Cherry burst and
That's the idea
You keep the hair
That you have
It's stronger
Than heredity

the big ten looks
terrible, jogger types
every proposition
braced on an emergency
animal rescue story:
what if we see an animal
in trouble? do what
you can to get
somewhere safe
then page me

Thus it is stronger
Than it is in
Morphoplasticism
I feel compelled
To admit that such
A clarification
Has led me with
Regard to the comp-
Licated progress
Of taking sides

passing through
several phases
gradually eliminated
descriptive elements
like his bleeding
necklace, and beans
do they really think
Silver may still be
sitting in his cage
waiting for us?

Silver was not
The only bird
Scaling the scaffolding
In a geometric
Progression
While cutting class
Ever had the price
Stamp come down
On your head
A photo can stomach it

the shopkeeper knew
I only bought
to legitimize our
entry into his store
while my friends
plundered the aisles
divorced from
the natural world
and formal code
kleptos in progress

Universality ignores Martians
I never sound that
Is how we have been
Accumulated drip stains
Services honestly, simply
Our direction has been
Absolutely forerunning
Slowed to foretrotting
Okapis on bivouac lane
View by dollar van

Staring at me, and
Only I ever seem to
See it. Greg may
No longer believe
The mouse is real
But, perhaps, a fig
Newton of my eviction
And his. Green ceiling
Goodbye forever
C-I-L the landlord

Parking lot spring-joy
In an alternate kite
Blows wig across
The promenade, deck
Patio, foyer, red cobra
Exhibit, the alligator
Snapping butterfly
Wing of powdered
Death buffet with
Chlorinated bath

that the real dying
took place between
surfaces, this drowned
man in a poem insists
through witness digging
by the shoreline
one experiences
a subjective beatdown
back home this mouse
was sitting on my bed

all year long I've been
trying to get the tone
wrong and winding
up forward, I'm way
ahead of my debts
headlights tumble
off the road, only
the steering wheel
survived, furry legs
race into restroom

what if I wake up
with the mouse in bed?
why has it come into
my life? I have no food
or time to bond, and
am in a state of forced
departure, cruel human
life awaits my future
in kinds of ballads and
drool called English, mouse

Artificial light turning
Business lunch workshops
Into s/m sock hops
Without admission
Round up wine
And boxes, oh fuck
Where is my Reed
Celibacy club T-shirt?
In a vessel terminating
In the head of a ram

my plan: rabid tax
exemption for
renewable energy
I was a small oil
person for awhile
all of a sudden
the problem of no
plan arrived, I'm
against removing dams
drilled on the base

For five dollars you
Can have a lunch at
A fine restaurant
And learn how to
Ten minute workday
First Poets Wanted
Sign sighted today
For battle between
Medgar Evers
And Baruch

as the visual henceforth
replaced quiver plaque
harbors evidence she
is shooting in the wintry
bedbug yippee! such
as the meeting soul
may pierce o cruel hands
the oily skin flick
across which many stolen
goods have been dragged

A stable strategy
Of keeling, face
Of Ernie, I walk
Where inculcate
Extremes sew on
Faces, Face of
Bert, lid (?) with
A serpent, thirty
Gold roundels
Of bulbous form

he wants to promote
a culture of life
but knows he must
change a lot of minds
to make it so, soft-
paste porcelain with
incised decoration
under creamy white
gauze, strict construct-
ionists on the bench

If you don't know
What you're supposed
To know we'll get to
You early before it
Gets late. I invited
The Prime Minister
Of Russia to my house
I shook my head as hard
As I could and watched
The little flakes swirl

one train another way
three walk through
one Good Friday
no comes a train
one apparently needs
a better commander
four leap over two
turnstiles, attempting
to crawl home via
early morning G-train

That gone shelf
That gone box
To speaking for
The so-called sane
Chucking rocks
Sixteen cops
And me writing
This on the train
Sharing lines
For several stops

the stuck train between
stations, absence
at job number two
for a drain, ribcage
outside its lines
paid to grade degrees
of freedom, if
accepted onto payroll
being my Dime's question
if I can afford its form

Sap the eel skin
Wallet, he believes
Genocide is a threat
To our national
Security generally
Speaking, white
Beans, turkey
Sausage at Tom's
He doesn't believe
Changing laws

and afterwards my poems
blew out the back of the car
in which we were speeding
today all my ideas are liquid
for instance, when Mr. Bump
was a bus driver he fell
off the bus and couldn't
catch up with it, and all the
passengers traveled for free
changes social policy

K is a supercluster
The good goo stew
Eyes, wrists, summits
Jaundice in uniform
Inside this vivid dot
Papers say deal with it
But you are side-by-side
The eviction and the blimp
Painting into office hours
And elegance gets taken

there to be owned
there wasn't anything
angle, don't reflect
growed up at an acute
where I appeared to
in the treeyard graveyard
tar wheezing capital c
if all is idyllic capital
so all may not claim
the wound he refurbishes

Video game B-15 bombers
Buzz overhead and this
Van leaps laying me
Out stomach pressed
To the interior roof
Albert, don't let
The back door open
Suddenly on horseback
Riding through caves
Wear shades to see vultures

but not their colors.
down a trail a war
party? mountainous
rock formations and
a little weigh station
we stay there long
enough to state our
intentions. "You never
know who might fall
on you around here

I camped inside a mt.
And forty men fell
Through its peak
They were with this
Blind painter who was
Working on the side
Of the mountain He
Had to carry 200 lbs.
Of painting equipment
Back on his own."

phone rings ending Al's
story. Piece some of it
back to tell his sister
eight positive trees
eight green-painted metal
positive trees fucking
in the positive distance
there was a time in my life
when I was just taste
a violent commencement

Free enterprise, I think
Would be very important
To God. Splat Pig
An unaccustomed event
The light of day
Cannot grant felicity
To the behavioral
Sciences. She might
Be hoping you aren't
Thinking of her, ever

yesterday the theological
feuds in the tavern
but today the snuggle
and although your
thoughts have never
amounted to much
watching you think
is a beautiful thing
in a ripped imagination
I am tampered with

New Jersey Transit style
Churlish and relaxable
When we feel or
Have an understanding
Me and repetition
Wasting conceits
Lilting rhododendrons
Umbilical hernia
Pushing Buttons
Totalitarian chic

their tones waxed loud
feeble insects made it
in the stormy sea
and paunch grown sleek
with sacrifice, as once
Electra her sepulchral urn
gone to Como they said
and I have posted to Como
bear markets to admire, bright
bow of that exhausted shower

But hanging chad
A break in the punch out
Does count. At first
It had to be hanging
Chad that let a pinhole
Of light shine through
But part way through
The count, the rules
Were changed to drop
The must-show-light rule

imagine that the presidency
could rest on
the difference between
dimpled chad
vs.
pregnant chad
like a gate closing
a hanging chad
can close the hole
if not punched cleanly

Inspiration technology
We no longer light up
Whichever chump winds
Up Prez, can't light up
Bulb or bong. HST
Ca. 10/72: "How
Low do you have to
Stoop in this country
To be President?" Closer
Vague, or reach in touch

honorable mention: place
having lacked anything
but love, and a roof
put the head down
that intense human
quality of holding
back at pivotal
moments, find and
replace, my heroes
have always been boxes

Ah you couldn't just
Let me go home. I
Had to not only
Show but say
Describe, denounce
That I might have
Anything to say
And still stand on
That absence of principle
You call a head

normative splotch, what
is the strategy of my address
we shall be called
purgers, then leave
him out, when the fit
gives myself a voluntary
wound, ravenous same
console, list of
larcenous queries, mark
stealer, back to back rack

In slack almanac slang
I couldn't help but feel
How unfair it was
For the animals. Again,
They were paying
The price for people
Being unprepared.
Lane divides ahead.
My favorite rhyme
Is unprepared and ahead

that was hairy and you
ammunition accessory
the panels said chewy
died saving others
on a rock breaking
in half while hurtling
through space, you
are the other art's
I isn't, hero grasping
ostrich turns corner

Room full of shadows
I like panoptical
Heavenly spleen
No galette
"There's a man going
'Round taking names"
Sweatlight through
DeGaulle shuttle
Windows, wake in
The roach arms hotel

Lie to the customs forms
Anti-capital cliché
Satisfied, gaunt fem
Socio-appropriate dark
No darkness, how do I
Go far enough and not
Dissolve, Doug's islands
Escort my heart
Out of Paris
Body drags along

"I'll give you half
Of everything I own"
Bursts of light fired
From a dark self-core
Rupture clarity, an open
elegy and a stranger
disagreed, Gazing into
his crystal diploma
of resistance, and a
whiskey-filled dixie cup

I'm having trouble attending
my job, though doing so
and getting things done
had the following dreams
that my back was deformed
because a limb started
to spring out from
the top middle part
and turned in on
itself, that Eddie

had a similar deformity
and looked good in a
t-shirt with it
that a nurse/poet
attending to HIV+
babies recognized me
on 14th St. but couldn't
leave a conversation
designed as an argument
for his patients

that millions of these
parti-colored, animated
circles popped into
existence in some
nightmare puke decor
living room we were
in, started growing
sharp teeth and we were
goners but they dumbly
kept endlessly colliding

That a poem being read
Was the texture of this
One dream, realized it
Was Doug's and woke
Feeling as if I'd just
Been told he'd died
Pitching well in
The modern era means
Minimizing the damage
This I on the record

Obliterated one dream
Entirely from memory
Total foliage to swallow
Ample belly space
For nesting, our mission:
Bring obituaries and
Selves to Golden's Bridge
Westchester, florentine
And blackstone eggs
Sawbuck for headphones

Grand Central breakfast
Permit, Pig chirping
In the shower, spiky
Damp feathers, denies
You a needle, cramlin'
Through the prairie
Near the off ramp
Mad country blanks
Severely altered
In a traditional manner

work vs. The Greatest
Of All Time: today
felt bad at first
then a little better
then worse than that
got to the office and felt
alright, but not so
good, later felt reasonably
good, but only after
a stretch of feeling

bad or not so good
felt ok for twenty minutes
then heavy in a less
than interesting way
for forty-five minutes
felt a little better after
that for a little while
things were good for
a few minutes after that
I didn't feel bad or good

for an hour. When
I left work I felt
drained, and blank
I drink because
I can't see in my
poems. The this and
that of a this and
that porn rugrat, everyone
feels good when
Kevin says "total sodomy"

Was that you plummeting
From the upper deck?
Boston inhales, at work
Faking functions, infinite
measure: hang it where
you stand when anything
happens. "As you can see
He is no longer there"
Why does it look like
Life is still in that body?

Gray Paris Good Friday
Land inside a reality
Pressed onto brain
By Doug's dying
Buyitbuyitbuyitbuyit
I trust this hotel's lack
Of quality, like a crazy
Old neighbor's daily
Arranging of trash cans
In front of the stoop

An attentive provider
Of surefire dystopic
Drive, I would like
To be wealthy enough
To buy back all of
My pictures and put
My foot through them
In a bad frame of mind
And that influences me
More dreams pour in:

searching through record
bins for Bessie Smith
albums with Doug and
Eddie, dinner rue des
messageries flat, Doug
fades out as the meal
starts; what can you
say about where you
are? Mojave desert
town ten weeks later:

asleep in great grandmother's
old bedroom, wake up
chilled and feverish
two blankets two aspirin
back in bed shivering
then walking to Buy Rite
for cigarettes half-mile
away, walk out into
July 2am eve, see neighbors
seeing snow strands fall

for the third time
in Needles history
long pieces of fallout
David who should be
in Kansas catches up
before I turn a corner
met at the house by
Reed Bye, who should
be in Boulder, give them
detailed explanation

Still chilled and burnt
Third time shock
Of dream state
Recognition of Doug's
Death as if it has
Just happened, wake
Up in great grandma's
Bed fever broken
Win sixty dollars at
Pioneer casino next night

so one becomes less
apparently visible
to break even for
the trip, or grows
larger as a letter
from Lyn puts it
broad winged hawk
over Bethlehem Steel's
dorm-like ghost, an
argument with space

Kindness acts unnaturally
However small the right
Island fell over the side
A boxer's sounds interrupt
Plosively, you could think
Of such a vast, flat
Body suffering, rights
Out to lease, but
That would be too easy
Mind a variation of harm

"keep thinking" one gets
told after a series of
misunderstandings gladdened
in a toy war of persons
left batty by unseen
selves, ash with stench
print this sea in case
you may have your wish
rub out the drawing
the hole at your feet

Half a historical prize
An ordinary flake
Donned folding space
Hear your lover's
Voice during a stroke
Miles away? "Ah'm
To suck your asshole
Stomp it, ain't mah
Style." Voice box
Spat, act in kind

laid his bird in down
I use his words
to propel mine through
every rank passageway
of this now sold off hotel
grey from the dressing
gowns, heron launches
high against empurpling
clouds, beamish and
speaking with humor

8/00 – 12/00

EDGE BOOKS

INTEGRITY & DRAMATIC LIFE Anselm Berrigan $10
SOME NOTES ON MY PROGRAMMING Anselm Berrigan $15
THEY BEAT ME OVER THE HEAD WITH A SACK Anselm Berrigan $5
CIPHER/CIVILIAN Leslie Bumstead $14
COMP. Kevin Davies $16
THE GOLDEN AGE OF PARAPHERNALIA Kevin Davies *forthcoming 2007* $15
AMERICAN WHATEVER Tim Davis $12.50
THE JULIA SET Jean Donnelly $4
LADIES LOVE OUTLAWS Buck Downs $6
MARIJUANA SOFTDRINK Buck Downs $11
CLEARING WITHOUT REVERSAL Cathy Eisenhower *forthcoming 2007* $14
METROPOLIS 16-20 Rob Fitterman $5
METROPOLIS XXX: THE DECLINE & FALL OF THE ROMAN EMPIRE Rob Fitterman $12.50
WORLD PREFIX Harrison Fisher $6
DOVECOTE Heather Fuller $14
PERHAPS THIS IS A RESCUE FANTASY Heather Fuller $14
NON/FICTION Dan Gutstein *forthcoming 2007* $14
SIGHT Lyn Hejinian and Leslie Scalapino $15
LATE JULY Gretchen Johnsen $3
ASBESTOS Wayne Kline $6
BREATHALYZER K. Silem Mohammad *forthcoming 2007* $14
THE SENSE RECORD Jennifer Moxley $14
DAY POEMS Mel Nichols $5
THE BEGINNING OF BEAUTY PART I Mel Nichols $10
STEPPING RAZOR A.L. Nielsen $9
ACE Tom Raworth $12
CALLER AND OTHER PIECES Tom Raworth $12.50
ERRATA 5UITE Joan Retallack $14
DOGS Phyllis Rosenzweig $5
INTERVAL Kaia Sand $14
ON YOUR KNEES, CITIZEN: A COLLECTION OF "PRAYERS" FOR THE "PUBLIC" [SCHOOLS] Rod Smith, Lee Ann Brown, Mark Wallace, eds. $6
CROW Rod Smith, Leslie Bumstead, eds. $6
CUSPS Chris Stroffolino $2.50
HAZE: ESSAYS POEMS PROSE Mark Wallace $12.50
NOTHING HAPPENED AND BESIDES I WASN'T THERE Mark Wallace $9.50

AERIAL MAGAZINE

(edited by Rod Smith)
AERIAL 10: LYN HEJINIAN co-edited by Jen Hofer *forthcoming 2007* $16
AERIAL 9: BRUCE ANDREWS $15
AERIAL 8: BARRETT WATTEN $16
AERIAL 6/7: FEATURING JOHN CAGE $15

Books published by Aerial/Edge are available through Small Press Distribution (www.spdbooks.org; 1-800-869-7553; orders@spdbooks.org) or from the publisher at PO Box 25642 • Georgetown Station • Washington, DC 20007. When ordering from Aerial/Edge directly, add $1 postage for individual titles. Two or more titles postpaid. For more information please visit our website at www.aerialedge.com.

010 0101010101000000000000000000

00000011111111111000101000111111111

11111111111000101010101111111111001

0101010101010101010101010101010101010101010

1010001010010100010000101000 1

11101010101001001000100100 01010

101101111111111010101010101010101001

0101010101010101010101010101010101010010

0101001010101010101010101010101010101001

0100101010101010101010010101010101001010

01010101010010101010101010101

10100110

010010000101010010101010101010100000001

11111111111111111111111111111111100000

1010101010101010101010101010101010101010

01010101010101010101010101010101010101010

010100101001010010001010010000000000

11111000111111

10101000100010

1010101010101010000000000000000000

0000000111111111110001010001111111111

11111111111100010101010111111111111001

1010101010101010101010101010101010101010

010100010100101000100001010001

111010101010010010001001000101 0

0101101111111111101010101010101010101001

1010101010101010101010101010101010010

1010100101010101010101010101010101001

10100101010101010101010100101010101001010

10101010101001010101010101

010100110

101001000010101001010101010101000000001

1111111111111111111111111111111111100000

1101010101010101010101010101010101010

1010101010101010101010101010101010101010

10101001010010100100010100100000000

11111000111111

10101000100010